the Companion DISCUSSION GUIDE for the ATF Teen Devo magazine

[Issue 1 • Volume 1]

Building the New Generation of Believers

COOK COMMUNICATIONS MINISTRIES
Colorado Springs, Colorado • Paris, Ontario
KINGSWAY COMMUNICATIONS LTD
Eastbourne, England

NexGen® is an imprint of
Cook Communications Ministries, Colorado Springs, CO 80918
Cook Communications, Paris, Ontario
Kingsway Communications, Eastbourne, England

THE COMPANION DISCUSSION GUIDE FOR THE ATF TEEN DEVO MAGAZINE
©2005 by Cook Communications Ministries

First printing, 2005
Printed in the United States of America
1 2 3 4 5 6 7 8 9 10 Printing Year 09 08 07 06 05

Editor: Mary Grace Becker
Cover Design: Brand Navigation
Interior Design: Helen Harrison (YaYe Design)

INTRODUCTION

Being a teen is hard. You, as their youth leader, know this. Making the grades, and succeeding in sports, work, and relationships, requires effort and a certain maturity and finesse. High expectations from parents, teachers, coaches—and unrealistic expectations from the media—make for a tricky road to maneuver. For many, just getting through high school with one's self-esteem intact is the ultimate survivor story.

Although all teens need friends, your role as youth leader needs to be much more. The key to working with teens comes down to this: care for them, listen to them and become someone they can trust and learn from. Above all, pray for them by name each week. Allow your teens to share their feelings without interrupting and analyzing their every word. An open heart toward them is the best gift you can give.

This companion 10-lesson Discussion Guide is for use with the *Acquire the Fire Teen Devo* magazine, Issue 1. Take time to familiarize yourself with the magazine before meeting with your group. The magazine's informal approach invites teens to look inside and discover God's wisdom, wonder, and love for them. The sessions in this discussion guide will allow you to help your teens get a handle on their thoughts and feelings and learn from the process of examining them.

Each session is divided into three sections: **Beginning, Middle,** and **End.** It doesn't get simpler than that! The **Beginning** may include an optional activity to grab the interest of the group. If you choose not to do it, go ahead with the lesson. It's your choice. Open with prayer asking God to unite your group, making your time together one of trust and concern for one another. After the prayer, move ahead to the discussion questions.

The **Middle** takes you into the heart of *Acquire the Fire.* Some sessions focus on segments in the Guys' section and others in the Girls' section of the devo. Have everyone in the group turn to the page and look at it together. Use the suggested questions to get the ball rolling. The **End** gives everyone a chance to reflect on how the issues you've raised affect each person individually. Close your time together with the prayer provided or use your own. Be sure to answer any questions your teens bring up.

Music is a must. Play it in the background or use it to accompany open prayer times. Food makes a great ice breaker, too. Leading a group of teens takes energy, attention, commitment, and a sense of humor. God applauds your effort with his teenagers, as do we!

Before You start,

here are the brief descriptions for the devotions found inside the Acquire the Fire Devo magazine. They expand on the five topics for Issue 1: love, friends, faith, the media, and worry. All of the devos below repeat in each section but vary by topic.

■ DEVO 1: Need2Know

This devo focuses on what the Bible says on the topic, the basic beliefs of Christians.

■ DEVO 2: MAN-datory

This devo reflects on what makes a godly man on fire for Christ.

■ DEVO [2]: girl-OUTstanding

This devo reflects on what makes a godly woman on fire for Christ.

■ DEVO 3: Godfidential

This devo is written by youth pastors and "twenty-somethings" who remember the struggles of the teenage years. Writings will inspire, encourage, and deliver Christian wisdom.

■ DEVO 4: Up/In/Out

This devo contains a Scripture passage that teaches a discipleship principle. UP–how it relates to our relationship with God; IN–How it relates to our relationships with others; and OUT–How it relates to our relationship with nonbelievers.

■ DEVO 5: Truth and Dare

This devo is divided in two; A "Truth" section–a Scripture passage related to the topic and a paragraph that ties the Scripture to today's teens. And a "Dare" section–strongly worded challenge to the teen to take the truth of the Scripture and stand up for Christ.

■ DEVO 6: Faith on Fire

How faith is key to dealing with each topic.

■ DEVO 7: The Super Natural Power of Prayer

Well-worded prayers for teens to use.

■ Generation MY

Christian girls answer teen questions.

■ Tribal Wisdom

Christian guys answer teen questions.

And there you have it! Lesson 1 is straight ahead.

4

GETTING BACK AND GIVING UP

Bible Truth:
Even when it's hard, love others.

Bible Verse:
"Do not seek revenge or bear a grudge against one of your people, but love your neighbor as yourself. I am the LORD" (Leviticus 19:18).

Stuff:
Bibles, something soft to throw (at least one per person). Beanbags, spongy balls, or newspaper wads taped together. If you have space outdoors and don't mind getting wet, use water balloons. (Note: Avoid "wet T-shirt contests." Girls may also be uncomfortable wearing wet shirts.)

LESSON ONE

BEGINNING

As you start your devotional time together, ask God to give you his wisdom while you journey through today's lesson. Invite members of your group to share prayer requests if they are comfortable doing so. Have one or two volunteers pray aloud for these requests.

Ask one of your teens to stand facing you, about an arm's length away. Say, **I'm going to do something rather unpleasant, and I want you to respond to what I'm doing with your first impulse.** Rap your finger on your student's upper arm—just hard enough to get his or her attention. Do this again two or three more times just to annoy him or her! Your volunteer's reaction will likely be to move away, tell you to stop it, or to thunk you back. Be prepared for a different reaction as well.

Ask the group: **How many of you thought Jaime** (substitute the name of your volunteer) **would tell me to stop or back off? How many of you thought he or she had good reason to get mad or retaliate?**

Optional Activity

Pull out the beanbags, spongy balls, newspaper wads, or water balloons and allow your group to use them to battle it out for a few minutes. (Note: Girls may be uncomfortable wearing wet shirts.) Watch and see if any of them resort to taking revenge against people who pelt them with the objects. After a couple of minutes, call a stop to the madness. Recap with some of your observations about the activity.

If necessary, make your point by saying, **When someone hurts us, our natural instinct is to strike back.** Ask for a show of hands from your teens if they empathize with any of the following scenarios: being shoved into a locker, being walloped in the head by a snowball, having their backpack stolen and the contents dumped out on the school's parking lot. Ask, **What happens to your gut when you experience something like that?** Pause. **Revenge is a powerful impulse.** Discuss.

Q. **When was the last time you wanted to get revenge? What did you do?**

A. How forthcoming teens are will depend upon how comfortable they feel with the group. Be open to listening to some fairly minor examples, knowing that your group will be thinking privately about more significant experiences. On the other hand, your teens may surprise you with bigger examples in an attempt to justify their actions.

Summarize this section by saying: **It's human nature to want to get back at others. If someone spreads a rumor about you, do you start a rumor back? If your dad says "No" to going to a party Saturday night, do you skip class on Monday just to get even with him? Let's look at what God's Word says about revenge and love—a very strange combination.**

MIDDLE

Have everyone turn to page 7 in the Guys' section of *Acquire the Fire, Issue 1.* Ask a volunteer to read Leviticus 19:18 from the "Up/In/Out" devo.

Q. Why can't we simply love others no matter what? What makes us want to seek revenge?

A. We want what we think is fair. We don't like feeling hurt, so we want the other person to hurt too. We automatically protect ourselves. Revenge feels good and seems justifiable. (Your teens may bring up some situations where they felt revenge was justified. Listen carefully and acknowledge their feelings without condoning any vengeful behavior.)

Q. If you carry a grudge but don't actually do anything about it, is that okay? Does it hurt anyone?

A. You hurt yourself when you carry a grudge because you are putting pressure on any goodness that might be tied to that relationship. You can also get so obsessed with your grudge that you lose perspective. It can become more important than it really is, taking your energy away from the things you should focus on. Carrying a grudge also hurts your relationship with God because you are doing something he doesn't want you to do by putting your will above his own. It gives Satan a lot of satisfaction to see Christians seething over seemingly minor offenses.

Ask a volunteer to read the "Up" section.

Q. On a scale of 1 to 10, how hard is it for you to do what God commands of you? Explain.

A. This can be really hard when our human nature cries out for payback. Sometimes if it's a small thing, we don't mind doing it. But if we've really been hurt, it's a lot harder to just set that aside. We want things to be fair.

God knows a lot more than we do about how our relationships will eventually turn out. Ask a volunteer to read the "In" section.

Q. If God knows the big picture of every relationship, why does he allow difficult ones to exist?

God knows a lot more than we do about how our relationships will turn out.

A. God doesn't control every choice we make or the people we come into contact with. He created each of us with a free will. Our human choices lead us to different kinds of people who are all making their own choices. Sometimes that adds up to tough relationships that we don't always understand. The important thing is to honor God in those relationships.

Q. Think back on a difficult relationship you've had. How did you become *better not bitter* as a result?

A. Sometimes the experience of a tough relationship teaches us something about ourselves that we really needed to learn. We're better equipped to handle difficult situations in the future and we learn about God's faithfulness.

Relationships are complicated. They are never "one size fits all." We have expectations and we make assumptions. It is easy for us to take people for granted or to be taken advantage of. All relationships grow and change, but it is important to remember that God is at the core of those relationships that honor him and put him first. Ask a volunteer to read the "Out" section.

Q. In what ways do Christians respond in ways that are not "Christlike"?

A. Doing things our way guarantees we get what we want momentarily, but it may be the worst thing we can do. We need to try to do what pleases God, not what pleases us or our friends. With God's help, Christians can respond to difficult times with faith in God and patience.

Q. Tell about someone you know who didn't try to get revenge for a situation that left *you* feeling angry. What were your feelings at first? Disbelief? Confusion?

A. Answers will vary. Follow up with questions about what made the difference for the person who didn't seek revenge.

Q. Many people hated Jesus as he went about his everyday life on earth. He was beaten, scourged, spit upon, shackled, and in his final days mocked and nailed to a cross. Although it was easily in his power to do so, Jesus did not exact revenge on his enemies. If you consistently follow Jesus' example, how will it change your relationship with your friends, your family, and people you don't necessarily get along with?

A. Ask this question in three parts (friends, family, and people you don't get along with) and encourage teens to give specific examples for each situation. (For example, giving people the benefit of the doubt or a second chance, etc.)

Back to our verse—not only does God not want us to take revenge; he wants us to *love* our neighbor. That means everyone we come into contact with. *Everyone.*

END

In the New Testament, loving your neighbor as yourself is a big deal. Jesus quoted this verse more than once. (Matthew 22:39, Mark 12:31 and Luke 10:27) **Paul quoted it as well.** (Romans 13:9 and

Galatians 5:14) **James did too.** (James 2:8) **Of course it's easy to understand the benefits when others love us. But doing good things for people we don't like or those who don't deserve it— now that's a different story.**

Yet, that's what God wants us to do—do things for others that show God's love. With God's help, we can love even the most difficult people in our lives. After all, it's not about us, but them. God wants us to die to ourselves daily (our wants, needs, desires, attitude). Sound impossible? Think of it this way. God loves you the imperfect being that you are—with all of your faults and bad habits. We're all sinful. Allow the Holy Spirit to shape you to be more and more like your Heavenly Father.

Ask everyone to turn to page 8, Guys' section. Read aloud together the poem, "Because God Loves You."

Q. **Which phrase from this poem means the most to you? Why?**

A. Let your group focus on any part of the poem. Look for ways to affirm their insights and build bridges to the challenge we all have to love others.

Close your time together with a prayer like this one:

Father, you know what each of us is like. You know when other people push our buttons. When those tough moments happen, help us to pause and take a deep breath so we can do what you want us to do. You are Lord and Savior and we want other people to know that by what they see in our lives. In Jesus' name, amen.

LOVE THE WORLD

Bible Truth:
Live out God's love.

Bible Verse:
"Guide me in your truth and teach me, for you are God my Savior, and my hope is in you all day long" (Psalm 25:5).

Stuff: Bibles, three chairs

Love

LESSON TWO

BEGINNING

As you begin your devotional time together, pray and ask God to give you confidence to speak on the topic of love in ways that reflect wisdom and honor him. Invite members of your group to share prayer requests if they are comfortable doing so. Ask one or two in the group to pray aloud for the requests that have been shared.

Read the question from "Generation MY," page 6 in the Girls' section of *Acquire the Fire, Issue 1*, p. 6.

My best friend is a Christian and so is her boyfriend. But they are getting way too attached to each other. They hang all over each other at school. I think I should say something about her priorities, but I don't want her to get mad at me.

Stacey (15)

Discuss:

Q. When we find ourselves on a "hot seat," that is, in a situation that conflicts directly with our Christian beliefs, how should we respond? Will a gentle response work better than an insistent or angry one?

Answers will vary.

Q. What do you think it means to speak the truth in love?

A. Being honest because you care about someone. Being careful about the person's feelings, but still saying what you need to say. Being bold enough to say what needs to be said even if that person doesn't want to hear it.

Optional Activity

Find out what your teens really think about a situation that conflicts with their Christian beliefs. Grab two or three hot headlines from an online site, blog, or local newspaper. Then set up three chairs in front of your group. Find two volunteers, a guy and a girl, and have them sit in two of the chairs. Leave the third chair empty. Say, **I'm going to read a real-life situation and the two in the "hot seats" get to tell us what they think about it. If anyone else wants to share an opinion, go and sit in the empty chair.**

Summarize by saying, we know God wants us to love others. Sometimes we just don't know how to go about it. Let's check out some hints.

MIDDLE

Ask everyone to turn to "Godfidential" on page 6 in the Girls' section of *Acquire the Fire*, Issue 1. Invite a volunteer to read this section aloud.

Q. Do you think love is a basic human need?

A. We all need love. This amazing quality (directly attributable to God) marks healthy relationships and makes the world environment a healthy, thriving community. Love also helps us go beyond our own needs to recognize the need in others.

Q. How can loving others eventually direct them to Jesus, even if we never say his name out loud?

A. Living out Jesus' love means doing it in a way that does not come natural to the world. People will notice that you're different—in a good way—and they'll wonder what makes you tick. Even if you never get a chance to explain about Jesus and God's love, you've planted a seed in that person's life.

Q. Christ wants us to love others as he loves us. What does that look like in real life?

A. Christ died for those who were his enemies. (Limitless love: love that sacrifices self for the sake of others). Jesus also loves us no matter what we do. That gives us a picture of forgiveness and acceptance of other people, even the ones who hurt us. Jesus loves us in a way that brings us closer to God, and our love for other people can bring them closer to God too.

Q. Answer the following statement with a "sometimes," "never," or "almost always." I feel incompetent when trying to show God's love.

A. We may look back on a conversation where we were trying to show love and fell miserably short. In such times, we have to take a step back and remember that God takes our imperfect offerings and works through them in his own perfect way. On the other hand, if we get too cocky about what we're doing, we forget that the real power comes from God. Maybe we try too hard because we want to bring attention to ourselves. It happens. When it occurs we have to move past it, and start anew.

Q. Although mistakes are hard to face, how can we learn from them and move ahead?

A. Self-reflection. We can admit it when we let self-interest get in the way and blur the picture. If we offend someone, godly understanding will teach us that the experience overall was more about "me" than "we."

Q. Are you ultimately responsible for whether someone believes in Jesus?

We can't argue someone into the kingdom of God.

A. We can't argue someone into the kingdom of God, nor can we love him or her in. It's the Holy Spirit's job to stir people's hearts. What you can do is plant the seed. That may be in the form of your faith, real-life experience, or passion. Each person must ultimately choose to respond to the Holy Spirit.

The "Godfidential" article gives us four BCs to help us show love in Christ's name.

Q. What does it take to be *convincing* when you want to demonstrate love?

A. You can act one way when you're trying to show love, and another way the rest of the time. But the action is phony.

Q. Why is it important to be *convicted* about loving others?

A. We can be convicted when we really believe in something and want to do it right. We can also be convicted in the sense that we know we haven't been showing love the way God wants us to. If we feel strongly motivated to share God's love, it becomes our new nature.

Q. What does it mean to be *consistent* in the way that you love others?

A. Again, we can choose to show love just to some and not to others. This is the way of the world today. People bump into each other, but never really connect. Consider loving others as a golden thread woven into who you are. It should be recognizable to all you meet.

Q. How does *compassion* show love?

A. Compassion means understanding the *feelings* of another. When we empathize with others, we better understand what they need. In such instances we put their needs above our own. Then we can respond in love by giving the right kind of help.

Ask a volunteer to read Psalm 25:5 aloud. "Guide me in your truth and teach me, for you are God my Savior, and my hope is in you all day long." **Even if we have the right motivation—to show God's love—we don't always know how to do it. This verse reminds us that we can ask God to guide us as we go about our lives. Opportunities unfold when we trust in him.**

END

If you looked up "love" in a Bible concordance you'd find columns and columns of Scripture verses that use the word. The Bible talks about love hundreds of times—God's love for us, our love for God, and our love for each other. In fact, love is right at the center of everything that God does, including giving his own Son for us (John 3:16). **Awesome!**

John was one of Jesus' closest disciples who went on to write the Gospel of John, the letters of 1, 2 and 3 John, and the Book of Revelation. He had tons to say about love.

Ask everyone to turn to page 13 in the Girls' section, "A Love Letter to Believers Everywhere." Ask a volunteer to read it aloud.

Q. What does this letter tell us about how important the true quality of love is to God and how important it should be to us?

A. God is love. He is the author or creator of love. Love starts with God. Because God loved us first, his love motivates us to love him in return and to love others selflessly.

God gives us friends and relationships, but we still have to remember that the most important relationship is the one we have with him. It is our jumping-off point. If we are centered in

him, we'll understand the difference between right and wrong, love and selfishness, and how to love those who seem impossibly annoying. We won't even have to ask *why we have to*, we'll just know.

Close your time together with a prayer like this one:

Loving Father, we often take your love for granted. We forget how pure, perfect and awesome it is. Help us to see the reminders you put in front of us throughout the day, and give us the courage to share its beauty and genuineness with others. In Jesus' name, amen.

FRIENDSHIP

Bible Truth:
Friendship is an excellent way to disciple for Christ.

Bible Verse:
"Accept one another, then, just as Christ accepted you" (Romans 15:7).

Stuff: Bibles, sticky notes

LESSON THREE

17

BEGINNING

As you begin your devotional time together, pray and ask God to guide you as you consider the value of friendships that honor him. Invite members of your group to share prayer requests if they are comfortable doing so. Have one or two volunteers pray aloud for these requests.

Optional Activity

Read each of the statements below. Ask your group to respond if they think the statement is true or false. Ask individuals for explanations to their responses. If you choose, write the statements on sticky notes and attach them to the backs of six in the group. Have others read the questions and the wearer respond true or false.

- **I expect that the friends I have today will be my friends 10 years from now.**
- **When you're not getting along, it's a sign that the friendship is over.**
- **If a friend makes you mad, forget about it. What's important is that the friendship remains intact.**
- **Being one way with one friend and another way with others is an acceptable way to hold onto friendships.**
- **It's normal for friends to come and go.**
- **It's important to have friends who support you even when you fail.**

Discuss:

Q. **What qualities attract you to someone new?**

A. Loyalty, support, common interests, someone to hang with, honesty, dependability, etc.

Q. **Is craving attention the same as seeking friendship?**

A. Craving implies an intense need. Friendships that start out with such an edgy beginning will most likely fail.

Q. **What happens when a friendship disappoints you? Does friendship involve a certain degree of risk?**

A. You might grieve the fact that things didn't turn out the way you thought they would. You might figure it wasn't meant to be and move on. If you got badly hurt, it might make you more careful when choosing friends the next time around.

Summarize by saying, We're social beings. God made us to need each other. We're hopeful that friendships work out. Let's take a look at God's perspective on friendship.

MIDDLE

Have everyone turn to "Need2Know" on page 14 of the Guys' section of *Acquire the Fire*, Issue 1. Ask a couple of volunteers to read this page aloud as everyone else follows along.

Q. Have you ever been treated badly by someone you thought was your friend? How did it feel? How did you respond?

A. If you were hurt, you might have withdrawn from the friendship. Or you might have become angry and lashed out.

Q. Have you ever known someone who wanted to be your friend, but you didn't really know why? Something about his or her approach made you uneasy. How did you respond?

A. If you're suspicious about a person's motives, your instincts may raise an alert; you might avoid them or act rude so they get the message that you don't trust them. At times, you might be surprised to find that you have a great deal in common after all.

The early Christians had good reason to be suspicious of a man named Saul. He was a devoted Jew, and he didn't like the idea of Jesus being the Messiah that the Jews had been waiting centuries for. So he made it his personal mission to persecute and imprison Christians. Then Jesus revealed himself to Saul on the road to Damascus and let him know exactly who he was. Saul got the shock of his life. In a heartbeat he became a new person, and he took on a new name—Paul. Paul was imprinted with a loving character because of the indelible impression Jesus made on his life. With the impact of God's love, Paul saw things in a whole new light—even though the experience left him blind.

Ask a volunteer to read Acts 9:11-15.

Q. Jesus told Paul to go find Ananias, a follower of Christ. What kind of welcome do you think Paul expected?

A. He probably figured Ananias would be afraid, angry and skeptical, but he also would have had the faith to trust that God would work things out. God really does change lives.

Q. The Lord told Ananias to put his hands on Paul's eyes to heal his blindness. How do you think you would have felt if you had been in Ananias's sandals?

A. You might have been reluctant, just like Ananias was, since you were in the presence of a passionate Christian-hater. Although you would have wanted to obey God, you also might have taken extra precautions to make sure you were safe. Your natural instincts would have collided with the obedience commanded of you by Jesus.

God really does change lives.

Paul spent a few days in Damascus and then headed to Jerusalem, where the inner circle of Christ's disciples had gathered. Above all, they were the ones who needed to be convinced that Paul had changed.

Ask a volunteer to read Acts 9:26.

Q. How hard is it for you to get past your first impressions, or to trust that someone has changed for the better? Explain.

A. This is very difficult to do. We want to protect ourselves from hurt and abandonment. We tend to form opinions quickly, leaving the person vulnerable to gossip and false judgments. If we've been offended or hurt by the person, it's even harder to believe that he or she has changed.

Ask a volunteer to read Acts 9:27.

Q. What might make you take the risk Barnabas did and stick up for an outcast?

20

A. A feeling that it's the right thing to do. A sense that doing this is what God wants you to do. A heartfelt desire to be fair.

Paul traveled thousands of miles on three major missionary trips. He traveled to Italy and Spain later in his life. Everywhere he went he welcomed people into the kingdom of God. And it all started with Barnabas accepting Paul and sticking by him when no one else would.

Q. What was the basis for Paul's quite unbelievable new attitude toward Christians?

A. He had been chosen and accepted by Christ himself, as awful and sinful as he was.

Q. Share with the group an experience where you felt accepted into a friendship or group—just the way you were—without having to fit in. Did you feel a sudden surge of confidence? Does unconditional friendship free you to look beyond your shortcomings to discover Christ's purpose for your life?

A. Answers will vary. Follow up with questions about how this experience of acceptance changed the teens who answer.

Q. Tell about an experience when you made an effort to accept or welcome a teen that your friends wanted nothing to do with. Did the friendship happen or did it eventually crumble under peer pressure?

A. Answers will vary. Follow up with questions about how this experience of offering acceptance changed lives.

Be open to friendship—that's the message here. It's the first step on the path to discipleship, that is, leading others to Christ. You never know where God will take you and your newfound friendships.

END

Have everyone turn to "MAN-datory" on page 19 in the Guys' section of *Acquire the Fire*, Issue 1. Ask a volunteer to read "MAN-datory" aloud.

The Bible character Joseph got a terrible deal from his jealous brothers. On top of that he got tossed into jail for something he didn't do. While in prison, he befriended a couple of men who got out before he did. They just happened to work for the king and promised to put in a good word for Joseph. But they never did—they left him hanging.

Q. With so many disappointments, how do you think Joseph felt about friendship overall?

A. He had good reason to doubt others' motives and intentions—including those people closest to him. But Joseph trusted that God had his best interest at heart even if it seemed very unlikely at the time.

Q. What can we learn about friendship from Joseph's story?

A. Above our worldly friendships, God promises us a relationship with him that is trustworthy and dependable.

God's friendship never disappoints. We live in his kingdom. He's with us all the time and knows everything we're going through. Even when the disappointment of other's leaves us directionless, hurt and confused, almighty God is a lasting friend.

Close your time together with a prayer such as this one.

The Bible calls Noah a friend of God. Lord, many of us find it hard to believe that the Creator of an entire universe would seek a friendship with sinful beings. But you do. In you, we understand the value and responsibility of friendship. But, we admit, that it's hard to be open and accepting of others for fear of being ridiculed and hurt. So we ask you to give us the strength we need to be true friends. You accepted us even when we didn't deserve it. Help us to show the same kind of openness to others. In Jesus' name, amen.

22

DEEP IMPACT FRIENDSHIP

Bible Truth:
Choose friends with care.

Bible Verse:
"He who walks with the wise grows wise, but a companion of fools suffers harm" (Proverbs 13:20).

Stuff: Bibles, poster board or newsprint, masking tape, markers

LESSON FOUR

BEGINNING

As you begin your devotional time together, be sure to pray and thank God for the deep, genuine friendships that have graced your life. Invite members of your group to share prayer requests if they are comfortable doing so. Have one or two of the teens pray aloud for the requests.

Optional Activity

Hang poster board or sheets of newsprint around the room. Say, **Let's continue our discussion on friendship. What do you think—are there different kinds of friendships? Is friendship dependent on a place or time? Can your school friends mix with your church friends? Do friendships formed on an overseas mission trip count as true friends even if you never see them again?** Have your group run a tally of the friends they've made in their neighborhoods, at school, church, work, through sports and clubs, etc. Discuss the results.

Discuss:

Q. Where are the places you first came in contact with your friends?

A. Answers will vary. Be listening for any patterns that you might want to come back to later.

Q. Was the meeting place important? Given the friend, would your friendship have formed anywhere?

A. Yes/No. Answers may include: true friends form a connection no matter the time or place.

Q. So would you say there are levels of friendship—or perhaps degrees of commitment within friendships?

A. Sometimes we learn the unspoken rules of how to behave in a particular environment, and we're that way only in that place. In another place we act and speak differently. In some situations there's not much time to talk individually, while in other situations you can talk a long time and get to know each other. Some relationships are based on what you do when you're together and don't go any further.

Say, **We meet people in lots of places. Most will remain just casual acquaintances. We know *of* them but not much *about* them. For example: think of the kids in your high school. Only a precious few will become core friends. Our discussion on friendship today really boils down to this: How can we be sure we're finding the friends of value that God wants us to have? And how often** do we let the distractions of shallow friendships lead us astray, compromising our connection to God?

MIDDLE

Ask everyone to turn to "Godfidential" on page 16 in the Girls' section of *Acquire the Fire*, Issue 1. Ask one or two volunteers to read this section aloud.

Q. Use your own words to define a "best friend."

A. Someone you can always count on. A person you enjoy spending time with. Someone who understands and accepts you—even with your weaknesses and failures. A person you don't have to prove yourself to. Someone you're comfortable spending time with even if you're not really doing anything but watching TV or hanging out.

Q. How do you think friendships shape the people we become?

A. We want to be accepted, so we do things that will help us fit in. That isn't always a wise choice. Teens can be desperate for acceptance from their peers. They fall prey to the false promise of approval at any cost. Downhill spirals can start slowly—the influence to do a little partying or the invitation to click on a porn web site, for instance. But small steps can lead to big ones. With true friends we're acknowledged and encouraged to stand up for what we believe, not judged for being different.

We may choose to think otherwise, but the people around us influence our behavior. We shop with people who like to spend money, eat with friends who enjoy a great pizza, study with people who are stuck on the same trig chapter, and party with people who know how to have a good time. Even such simple contacts can eventually lead us away from Christ. It's that simple. And it happens with our eyes wide open. Let's look at a verse about choosing friends.

Ask a volunteer to read Proverbs 13:20.

Q. Do your friends make godly choices? Why should you care?

A. Friends who seek God's truth make good choices. They know what they believe and they stick to their values. They want to please God in the things they say and do—even if they stumble and fall short. They don't make you do things you're uncomfortable doing.

Q. You're old enough to choose your friends. So how can you get hurt by mixing with the wrong crowd?

A. You can develop habits or attitudes that are destructive and steer you away from your passion and purpose in life. You get into legal trouble. You also could get hurt emotionally, physically, and financially if you are rejected or betrayed by people you thought were your friends.

Friends who seek God's truth make good choices.

Q. Does this verse mean that we should avoid non-Christians?

A. No. We're commanded by Jesus to spread God's love to non-Christians. But we have to be careful about who is influencing whom. A bad pull in the wrong direction is deceptively easy to walk into and difficult to draw away from.

God wants us to reflect his light in a dark world, not let the darkness consume the light. When on earth, Jesus walked a hard road. He was fully aware of the evil around him. For example, the Canaanite people indulged in crude sexual behaviors with prostitutes, worshiped pagan god and goddesses, and offered their children in sacrifice in the name of religion. Jesus was not immune to the sight of bloody crucifixtions that lined the road to Jerusalem or the terror and brutality of Roman soldiers that sought to imprison him and his friends. Yet, even with all this, Jesus' godly character was clear to see. And his disciples took notice and treasured his faith and friendship.

Q. Tell about an experience when you stood up for what you believed in. What difference did it make to you? What difference did it make to the people around you?

A. Answers will vary. Help your group identify the deep positive feelings that they and others had and any long-term effects it had on their friendships.

Q. How do you feel when you're in a situation that you know is trouble, but you don't do anything about it?

A. Answers will vary. Help teens identify that such uneasy feelings shoot up red flags that they need to identify. Discuss such instances: what they're doing with their friends and what options they have to respond: speak up, walk away, talk to someone. More often then not, there is something that you can do.

Close friends make great go-to Christians when doubt and trouble find us.

True friends help us stand up for the truth and help us become influencers, rather than go-along-with-the-crowd followers. In John 15:15, Jesus called his disciples his friends—an amazing statement.

Q. In what ways do your closest friends help you be more like Jesus?

A. Christian friends who are walking in faith give us great examples to follow. They encourage us to make the right decisions. Close friends make great go-to Christians when doubt and trouble find us.

Q. How does your relationship with God affect your choices in friends?

A. If you want to please God, you want to choose friendships that honor him and bring you closer to him.

END

Ask the group to turn to page 23 in the Girls' section of *Acquire the Fir,* Issue 1.

Q. According to this verse, how should we be praying for our friends?

Prayer
is a gift you give
to those you love.

A. For God to be at work in their lives. To request God's energy behind everything we do. For what we do to really count for God's kingdom.

Q. If you knew that your friends were praying for you, how would that affect your outlook on your day?

A. Answers will vary. Help teens focus on the encouragement that comes from knowing someone is praying for them.

Close your time together with a prayer such as this one:

Lord, we learn from you how to be a true friend. Help us to form friendships that also strengthen our faith and extend our outreach to the unbelieving world. Let us remember that you are the God of land and sea and the billions of stars that grace the night sky. All things are possible with you—that includes friendships with difficult people. In Jesus' name, amen.

Encourage teens to commit to pray for each other by name this week.

DOUBLE DARE FAITH

Bible Truth:
Be bold in faith.

Bible Verse:
"And without faith it is impossible to please God, because anyone who comes to him must believe that he exists and that he rewards those who earnestly seek him" (Hebrews 11:6).

Stuff: Bibles, half sheets of red and green construction paper

LESSON FIVE

BEGINNING

As you begin your devotional time together, pray and ask God to help you understand the true importance of having a bold faith. Have members of your group share prayer requests if they are comfortable doing so. You may also want to have one or two volunteers pray aloud for these requests.

Optional Activity

Pass out half sheets of construction paper, one green and one red, to each in the group. Ask everyone to close his or her eyes. Say, **I'm going to ask a few "Would You Dare?" questions, and I want you to hold up the green paper if you would take the dare and the red one if you wouldn't. Be honest. No one else will see what you're choosing.** Read the following questions.

- **Would you dare to join an outreach group that made it a habit to go door-to-door inviting people to your church?**
- **Would you dare to put your hands together in the school cafeteria and thank God for your lunch?**
- **Would you dare to speak up when a friend says God is just a fairy tale?**
- **Would you dare to tell strangers on a hiking trip how you became a Christian?**
- **Would you dare to offer to pray with a parent whose son was badly hurt in a drinking-and-driving car accident?**
- **Would you dare to write an essay for your school newspaper defending your faith?**

Ask students to open their eyes. Collect the construction paper. Say, **These are questions that cut to the heart of our faith. We have to look deep within ourselves to understand our answers.**

Discuss:

Q. Would you say 90 percent of the people who know you know you're a Christian? Come up with a percentage that reflects the right number.

A. Answers will vary. Teens who attend Christian schools, for instance, may answer, "yes," more readily than those who attend public schools. Answers may also depend on how closely tied your group is to the local church and whether they go to church and school together. But no doubt, they will think of plenty of people who do not know at all that they are Christians.

Q. Why do we as Christians feel uneasy about sharing our faith?

A. It's hard to be different. Some people like to make fun of anything religious. Faith is hard to explain. We might not be sure exactly what we are supposed to believe about our faith or know the Bible well enough.

Q. Does anyone have an extreme faith story to share? How did it change your life?

A. Answers will vary.

Say, **This isn't just a teen problem. Many adults have a difficult time putting their faith on display for unbelievers to see. They do the right thing and honor God with their lives, but they get a little weak-kneed if they have to explain their relationship with Jesus to someone who doesn't know him.**

When you feel fearful in your witnessing, it is a good idea to stop and ask yourself if maybe you are the one who is making it harder than it has to be. Sum up what you believe in one or two sentences. Then go ahead and practice saying your "mission statement" aloud while looking at your reflection in a mirror. Your confidence will grow as you learn to trust yourself with Christ's message. People often respond positively when introduced to Jesus, and you won't know how they'll react unless you try. Many unbelievers have been known to say that they never quite understood why it took a Christian so long to make the first move.

MIDDLE

Ask everyone to turn to "Truth and Dare" on page 32 in the Guys' section of *Acquire the Fire,* Issue 1. Ask someone to read aloud the "Truth" box.

Q. Tell about a time when someone asked you why you believe in Jesus. What did you say?

A. Experiences will vary. Encourage the teens to be honest about how they felt in the situation. Knowing that they are not alone in their feelings may actually encourage them to be bolder the next time they have an opportunity to share their faith.

Q. Does the story of Noah and the rainbow help you share your faith more confidently? Is the God of Noah's time the same God today? Why or why not?

A. It's a reminder we can see with our eyes. It's God's promise and God always keeps his promises. He promises to be with us everywhere we go and to help us know what to say. We can depend on that if we get into a conversation about faith that we're not sure we can handle. God is unchangeable, the same today, yesterday, and a thousand years to come.

Q. How can you tell if your "faith muscles" are stronger and more fully developed than last year?

A. Increases in physical fitness build endurance and strong muscles. You find yourself able to do things you couldn't do before, certain activities that used to make your muscles hurt are comfortable now. You breathe easier. The same holds true with Christian faith. You might even start doing some things automatically and not even have to think about your faith muscles. Like praying when people are around or talking about your church openly, or thanking God for his blessings.

Faith is a mysterious thing. When you have faith, it's real. It's a force or power that propels you to action. But if you don't have it, it seems strange to believe in something you can't see or touch. When you think of it, though, we do that all the time, don't we? We have faith that everyday things will happen—the sun will rise, there will be plenty of oxygen to breathe, our hearts will continue to beat steady and strong. And don't we also have faith in the promises and love of others?

Ask a volunteer to read aloud the "Dare" box.

Q. In what ways would you like to be more prepared to share your faith with other people?

A. To be more confident about what the Bible says and to know where to find the right verses. To be more knowledgeable about basic Christian beliefs and to be able to explain the hard things in the Bible. To practice knowing what to say before the situation arises so we don't sound foolish.

Q. What's the difference between witnessing and being witnesses?

A. Witnessing sounds much like an activity that you can start doing at a point in time, and then stop doing later. It's easy for us to separate that from "real life" and shove it into a religious corner. Being witnesses happens when we have Jesus living inside us, helping us to be more like him. It's not a religious thing; it's a way of life.

Q. How can you serve God so that he might use you to help other people come to know him?

A. Your willingness to learn more about Jesus and to speak up about your faith. An effort on your part to form friendships with people who may be ready to listen to what you have to say about God. Developing traits that make it easy to get to know people. Using your talents, like sports or music, that put you within easy reach of others.

When we seek God, our reward is an intimate relationship with a super natural power.

Q. What can you do in the next ten days to become better equipped to share your faith?

A. Offer your fear and excuses to God. Meet with a friend to pray and continue to support each other all week long. Choose a person to share with and pray for God to prepare that person's heart. Find a group to study the Bible with. Encourage teens to come up with something specific.

Read the verse at the top of the page again. **God wants a personal relationship with you, one that is active and dynamic, alive and well, and full of promise and hope. The verse states that God rewards those who sincerely seek him. When we seek God, our reward is an intimate relationship with a super natural power. His Spirit becomes closer to us than the breath that fills our bodies. Sometimes we meet people who seek God but are not ready to trust him with their belief. Nonetheless, even if they're not ready to take the full leap of faith, we can encourage others not to give up. If they continue to seek God, the Bible says they will find him.**

END

Have everyone turn to page 31 in the Guys' section of *Acquire the Fire*, Issue 1. Have volunteers read the two prayers aloud.

Q. Which of these prayers sounds the most like you? Explain.

A. Prayer is a personal expression, but be open to teens who are ready to talk about the insecurities described in these prayers.

Read Colossians 3:17 in the prayer box.

Q. How does Colossians 3:17 help strengthen our faith?

A. This verse reminds us of our true motivation for for the life we lead. Whatever we do, whether sharing about Jesus with words or modeling the attitudes of Jesus, we do it because we want to thank God for what he has done for us.

Let's take a few minutes to offer our own prayers. Be honest about the things that are tough for you when it comes to sharing your faith, or even letting people know that you're a Christian. Wait for the room to get quiet, and allow some time for silent, personal prayer. If members of your group know each other well, you may want to have them pray out loud together in small groups.

After a few minutes, end your time together with a prayer like this one.

Lord Jesus, we do not want to be pulled from the core purpose of our Christian lives. You are the best thing that has ever happened to us. And you don't ask us to keep you a secret; you ask us to spread the word! Instill confidence so that our faith flows from our tongues effortlessly and without embarrassment. Lead us to the people you want us to share with, and silence the fear when those big moments come. In your name we pray, amen.

FAITH BUILDERS

Bible Truth:
Put your faith to work.

Bible Verse:
"To all who received him, to those who believed in his name, he gave the right to become children of God" (John 1:12).

Stuff: Bibles

BEGINNING

As you begin your devotional time together, pray for God to give you discernment for his truth and a desire to develop a closer relationship with him. Invite members of your group to share prayer requests if they are comfortable doing so. Have one or two in the group pray aloud for the requests that have been shared.

Read the following statements and ask teens to indicate whether they agree or disagree. Encourage explanations.

- *Spirituality is a private matter.*
- *It doesn't matter what you believe as long as you believe something.*
- *If we want people to accept our religion, we should accept theirs, too.*
- *Anything you do to get close to God is spiritual.*
- *Religion and spirituality are the same thing.*
- *You can be spiritual without being religious.*
- *Your spiritual life is completely separate from your physical life.*
- *Feelings indicate the depth of your spirituality.*

Discuss:

Q. Do you have friends or relatives who practice different faiths?

A. Some teens may be curious to know people of other faiths so they can talk to them about their own faith. Others may see religion as part of culture and feel like certain groups of people are not likely ever to become Christians. Some teens may be uncomfortable outside their own circle and what they know well, especially if a person of another faith is outspoken and knowledgeable. No one wants to get trapped in a conversation they aren't ready for. Some may even question whether one religion is right and all the others wrong and ask whether Christians really have a right to force their views on others.

Q. Do you think of your faith in Jesus as something you do alone or something you do with others?

A. Individuals have to believe in Jesus for themselves, but God created us as social beings who need each other. Spending time with other Christians encourages us to grow in our faith. The New Testament has a lot to say about the Body of Christ and how we serve each other through prayer and in faith. Prayer and faith go hand-in-hand. When Jesus prayed it was physical.

MIDDLE

Ask the group to turn to "Need2Know" on page 24 of the Girls' section of *Acquire the Fire,* Issue 1. Have one or two volunteers read this section aloud.

Q. **What do feelings have to do with your faith?**

A. Emotions are sometimes an expression of our faith— whether weak or strong. But emotions and faith are not the same thing. How you feel inside is not what builds your faith. You can feel great, full of faith, and then when the tough times come, your faith crumbles. Or you can have great faith even when you feel overwhelmed by circumstances. Deep faith can be shaken but never completely extinguished. Know what you believe.

When Jesus prayed it was physical.

Q. **How much does what you do for others on any given day have to do with faith?**

A. The disciple James said faith without action is dead faith. If our faith in Jesus is really at the center of who we are, that will show in our actions. We'll do the things he wants us to, and minister to other people in his name. We won't just preach at them, we'll really care about them.

Turn to Matthew 14:22–33 in your Bibles and have volunteers read the passage aloud. **When his disciples were most afraid, Jesus said, "Take courage! It is I. Don't be afraid."**

Q. **How did this direct and personal encouragement from Jesus affect Peter's faith?**

A. Peter realized that because it was Jesus on the water, anything could happen. Even he could walk on water without being afraid. Jesus' comforting message encouraged Peter to stretch out his legs—literally. All the other disciples were terrified, but Peter saw an opportunity for faith. He was ready for an experience that no one else was ready to try or had even thought of.

Q. What happened to Peter's faith when fear got the best of him?

God always gives us another chance to focus our eyes on him.

A. He let what he was feeling—fear—determine his actions. He started out with great intentions, but as he quickly found out, intentions are a leaky vessel when compared to the sure-footedness of faith. But Peter didn't give up on faith completely. He reached out to Jesus and called on him to save him. He still believed. When we falter, that doesn't mean our faith is over or we're terrible Christians. God always gives us another chance to focus our eyes on him.

Q. What happened to the faith of the other disciples because of what they saw?

A. They saw Jesus in a way they had never seen him before. They called him the Son of God, which meant that they understood who he really was. Then they worshiped him. Faith lets us see who Jesus really is, and then we can't help but worship him.

Q. When Peter stepped out of the boat, he was making a conscious effort to exercise his faith. What situations propel you to take the risk and exercise your faith?

A. Answers will vary. Encourage your group to be specific. Rather than saying "school," for instance, help them recount a specific situation at school that stretched their faith. Focus on the point that we can make a choice to exercise greater faith. Some may have incredible stories to tell that can encourage the others in the group. Don't hesitate to share a story of your own.

Q. What sometimes causes your faith to "wrinkle" the way Peter's did?

A. When things don't work out the way you want. When a situation is too tough to figure out. When you're trying really hard to believe, and things still go to pieces. When bad things happen that you really can't understand, like a death or serious illness. When you are humiliated because of your faith. When something in the Bible doesn't make sense to you.

Q. Share a personal story where the simple yet amazing faith of another helped strengthen your own.

A. God may work in someone else's life in a way he hasn't worked in your life. Then you get to see something great apart from your own experience.

END

Ask the group to turn to "Top Ten Faith Builders" on page 33 in the Girls' section of *Acquire the Fire,* Issue 1. Have a different person read each one. After each one, have teens give a quick show of hands to indicate if that item is something they're interested in trying.

Q. Which items on this list would you recommend to your best friend? Why?

A. Answers will vary. Encourage your group to speak from personal experience as much as they can. As they hear each other talk about their experiences with some of these activities, the ideas will seem less like words on a page and more like something that can really be done.

Q. What does it mean to take a leap of faith (number 1)?

A. To put human sensibilities aside and simply believe. You believe in who God is, not in something human or physical—it's not the same as jumping out into nothing. You trust that God is there to catch you. A leap of faith may be a giant step forward in how you express your faith.

In Scripture, two words describe faith best: certainty and hope. "Now faith is being sure of what we hope for and certain of what we do not see" (Hebrews 11:1). Faith begins when we believe that God is who he says he is and that he'll do what he says he'll do. Jesus said "come" and Peter stepped out onto the water. Even when Peter's faith faltered and he began to sink, he knew he could call out to Jesus and Jesus would save him. The more experience we have with Jesus pulling us out of the turbulent times, the more certain we are that he's there.

Close your time together with a prayer like this one:

Lord, we're amazed at who you are and what you do for us. Too often our doubts get the best of us and our faith takes a dive. Pull us up out of the water as many times as it takes. We know that you are the Son of God. Supercharge our faith and fill us with the knowledge of your glory. In Jesus' name, amen.

FREE TO CHOOSE

Bible Truth:
Find out from God—not the world—how you should live.

Bible Verse:
"Consider how the lilies grow. They do not labor or spin. Yet I tell you, not even Solomon in all his splendor was dressed like one of these" (Luke 12:27).

Stuff: Bibles, index cards, pens

BEGINNING

AS you begin your devotional time together, pray and ask God to teach you to evaluate the negative impact that the media has on your life. Invite members of your group to share prayer requests if they are comfortable doing so. Have one or two volunteers pray aloud for the requests that have been shared.

Optional Activity

Find out what your teens really think about a difficult situation. Hand each student an index card and a pen. Say, **I'm going to read a scenario aloud and I want you to write a response as if you were an advice columnist for a Christian newspaper.**
Read this brief scenario and give the kids a chance to write a response.
Jake's mom shakes her head. She cannot believe the movie her sixteen-year-old son is watching on cable television. The bloody violence and the erotic sex scenes make it one of the worst she has ever seen. "It's just a movie," Jake mumbles between mouthfuls of popcorn. "It's not like I really would do any of that stuff."
Ask volunteers to read their answers.

Discuss:

Q. How much does what you see on television or on the big screen influence the way you think?

A. Some teens will undoubtedly say that they think for themselves and that what they see in the media doesn't really influence them. Others will admit that media images affect how they think about the way they look, making them feel like they have to look better in order to fit in. Visual images make powerful connections to the brain. What we see around us slowly begins to feel normal, even if it was unacceptable to begin with.

You might remind your group that much of what they see in the movies and on TV would have shocked viewers just a few years ago. Mention that when TV sitcoms first began, even the actors who were portraying *married* couples had to be shown sleeping in separate beds. Think of how things have changed. This can lead to a discussion about the influence of the media.

Q. How much does what you see on TV, in the movies, or in magazines influence how you spend your money?

A. According to an article in *The Cincinnati Post,* the average teen spends about $100 a week, with high schoolers averaging $1,400 a year on clothes, shoes, and accessories. Many of the items they buy are expensive because the media says that they're valuable—a name brand or designer label. The media is a big influence on spending habits of teens. How would the teens in your group say they compare to the national trend?

MIDDLE

Have everyone turn to "Balancing Your Wants and Needs" on page 41 of the Guys' section of *Acquire the Fire*, Issue 1. Ask some volunteers to read the article.

Q. **If you were left to survive on a deserted island, what one item would you take with you?**

A. Some teens will be practical and try to narrow the choices down to one thing they can get the most use from. Others will choose a sentimental item that they can't imagine living without. Others might say they would take something quite impractical, perhaps as a statement that they're tough and can handle anything.

Q. **What one thing on your real-life wish list would make your life easier?**

A. Cars may be at the top of the list, especially if you have older teens in your group. Teens who share a room with a sibling may wish for their own room. They may mention comfort items, such as a new sound system, or maybe their own credit card. Whatever the answers, encourage teens to be specific about the ways these items would make their lives easier.

The media in all their forms try to convince us of what we need. And when we see that other people have the latest stuff, we want it all the more. We don't want to be left out. But it's worth our while to consider why we respond to media the way we do. We wouldn't give control of our lives to anyone. Yet, we are left to internalize the images and advertisements we see without giving them a second thought. Think on this: Judges and lawyers in courtrooms across the country are becoming more and more concerned with the influence that TV crime show dramas have on today's jurors. It seems real-life jurors expect the legal process, as well as the discovery of evidence, to work much like they see on television.

Q. Describe a persuasive ad you've seen in the last week. What makes it so powerful and memorable?

A. Your group will probably mention current ad campaigns aimed at young buyers. Ads showcasing beautiful people in exotic places or engaged in exciting activities—and excelling at them. But they present these images in a way that suggests that anybody watching them can be just as beautiful and successful, which the average person quickly finds out is not true no matter what products are bought.

Q. How do you respond to these powerful ads? What about humorous ads? If the ad portrays men as inept fathers or blonde women as flighty, is there a problem?

Even without the expensive stuff, God promises to take care of us.

A. Responses will vary. Most teens likely will say that the ads don't really influence them all that much because they see right through them. But some will admit that the ads make them feel inferior in some way or will make them look at others in a degrading way. Some may say that ads give them something to shoot for, so they know what's "in", but that they can achieve the same look without spending so much money.

The Scripture passage in this article, Luke 12:27–31, reminds us that God will take care of us. We get way too hung up on whether we're going to have this or that—things that we'd like but that we don't necessarily need. Even without the expensive stuff, God promises to take care of us. He understands our needs.

Q. Why is it so hard to remember the truth of these verses?

A. We don't know the verses in our hearts. We get caught up in the world around us. We live in an independent society where we are taught to take care of ourselves. We don't stay close enough to God.

Q. How do you know your "stuff" limit? Do you know instinctively when enough is enough?

A. From a practical standpoint, you have too much stuff when you have nowhere to put it! But you can have too much stuff way before you reach that point. You may realize that you have a lot of things you haven't used in a long time. Sometimes the experience of being with a family who doesn't have as much or going on a missions trip where you see poor people who are nevertheless content is convicting.

Q. What can you do to make sure that what you see in the media are not defining who you are or determining your priorities?

A. Give some stuff away. Evaluate the value of each item in your life. Find someone who can get more use out of things than you can. If you're not ready to give things away, try boxing them up and putting them in the garage for a while. How long will it take before you miss having them around? You might not think about them for a lot longer than you think. Another idea is to make a decision to use money differently—give to a worthy cause, be generous with friends, save more for future goals.

END

Have everyone turn to "Free to Choose" on page 35 of the Guys' section of *Acquire the Fire*, Issue 1.

Q. What is the main point of this devo page?

A. It's a call to live an authentic life, without any of the half-truths that the media puts in front of us all the time. A lie is a lie no matter how you slice it. God made us each unique, and we don't have to spend our lives trying to be like the media says we should be.

Q. How can you apply these words to your life this week? In other words, how can you take back your life in Christ?

A. Answers will vary. Encourage the group to be specific about what action steps they can take.

Close your time together with a prayer like this one.

Father, we hear so many voices around us competing with your spiritual whispers and commandments. It's hard to shut them out. We want to hear your voice above everything else so that we choose what's right, fair, good, and outstanding in your eyes. In Jesus' name, amen.

EYES WIDE OPEN

Bible Truth:
God's ways come first.

Bible Verse:
"Whoever loves money never has money enough; whoever loves wealth is never satisfied with his income" (Ecclesiastes 5:10).

Stuff: Bibles, ads, books, CD covers, product packaging that targets today's teens. (Or take it a step further and collect products or material from when you were a teen. Have the dated material impact your kids. It was at one time "hot" and very cool!)

LESSON EIGHT

BEginning

As you begin your devotional time together, pray and ask God to help you evaluate the impact of the entertainment you watch in our highly visual world. Invite members of your group to share prayer requests if they are comfortable doing so. Have one or two in the group pray aloud for the requests.

Optional Activity

Display your collection of ads and packaging material. Have individuals in your group identify specific elements in the packaging that are aimed at teenagers. Evaluate their effectiveness. Why does the marketing campaign include them? What do the advertisers hope to accomplish? How successful do your teens think each ad is in influencing them?

You might think that you're in charge of all that goes into your brain. But there are others who would like to get a hold of it as well. In stealthy and subtle ways, advertisers look for the hook that will reel you in. More than that, they try *repeatedly* to get to you. Now is a good time to consider how successful they are.

Discuss:

Q. How susceptible do you think you are to the influence of media and advertising? Does it bother you to know that commercials steer your thinking in predetermined ways?

A. Answers will vary, but in general people don't want to admit they are as susceptible as they really are. Ask teens to give examples that support their claim that they are able to resist the pull of the media.

Q. On a scale of one to ten, how mindful are you about the effects of the movies and shows you watch? Do your preferences differ from your friends? Explain.

A. Answers will vary. In some homes, parents may still set the guidelines for TV and movie viewing. Older teens are more likely to make choices for themselves. They may push the envelope with the appropriateness of some movies as a statement of their maturity and independence. Ask a follow-up question that encourages your group to explain what their standards are for movie and TV viewing.

MIDDLE

Have the group turn to "Truth & Dare" on page 42 in the Girls' section of *Acquire the Fire*. Ask a volunteer to read aloud the Truth section.

Q. Do you think it's acceptable for companies to aim their marketing campaigns at teenagers? After all, isn't their primary aim to make money and not to help you? Or can it work both ways? Give an example.

A. This is a matter of opinion. On one hand, if teenagers are going to spend money, companies figure they might as well get a piece of the pie. On the other hand, teenagers are handling money for the first time, and the media makes it easy for them to make bad choices and get into financial trouble. Listen carefully to how your group answers this question to get a feel for how they feel about the media's influence and money in general.

Q. Do you have guilt over the amount of money you spend each month?

A. Some teens live on an allowance, and others have money to burn. Some are responsible for their own clothes, gas, lunch money, etc., while others are still used to their parents covering for those items. No matter how much they have, it's worthwhile to evaluate. Regardless of how much money they have, the question is whether teens are making wise choices with it.

Many of us consider money a private issue. It's not considered polite to ask someone how much money they make. Churches keep confidential the amount of donations people give. It's tacky to ask how much someone paid for a new house, new car, or some other high-end possession. Money habits start early, and advertisers know that. Guess what? They've had their eye on you since you first learned how to walk.

Ask a volunteer to read the "Dare" section of page 42.

Q. What do you think about this money challenge? How hard would it be for you to take the challenge?

A. Most people, even adults, spend a lot of money they can't account for—a latte here, a new CD there, lunch out, a shirt on sale at the mall. They're all small items individually, but they add up. Your teens might not think this is true of them, but challenge them to find out.

Q. If you had to justify the way you spend your money, could you?

A. Some teens are accountable to their parents; many others are not, and it would be unusual for peers to challenge the way their friends spend money. As they respond to the question, listen for what standards they set for themselves that set them apart from others.

Draw attention to the verse in this paragraph, Ecclesiastes 5:10.

Q. What truth does this verse hold for you?

A. Money defines priorities. No matter how much you have, you always want more.

Q. How can a person with a lot of money use it in a way that honors God? Can it really be done?

A. The obvious answer is to give money to the church and other Christian organizations. A less obvious answer is to live modestly despite having enough money to live well, or perhaps give anonymous gifts to people in need without even expecting a tax deduction out of it. What other ideas do your teens have?

Point out the definition of "greed" at the bottom of the Truth & Dare box.

Q. How often do you think about greed and whether or not it applies to you? Do you consider greed an old-fashioned idea?

A. Most of us would never want to admit we've been greedy. We're really good at coming up with reasons why we need stuff. If we thought about it more often, we'd probably think twice about some of the things we buy.

Q. Imagine living on a remote island without movies or TV or access to cable or satellite dishes. The island does, however, have plenty of shops and stores. Would the way you spend your money be different without the media's influence?

A. We might never think of a lot of the things we spend money on if the media weren't displaying images for us to crave. We would probably be more conscious of just using money for the things we need. We would spend on what we need rather than what we're told we need.

All of us manage to justify some pretty outrageous purchases, no matter what age we are. Spending is not just a teen issue. It is a culture issue that determines our life choices.

END

Have the group turn to page 43 of the Girls' section of *Acquire the Fire*, Issue 1. Read the poem aloud together or have a volunteer read it.

Q. What does the phrase, "I'm not for sale" mean?

A. I'm a real person. I'm not some image that the media dreamed up. You can't make me want to be like that. I'm not going to give in to your pressure.

Q. What other description of yourself would you like to add to the end of this poem?

A. Answers will vary. Encourage teens to be specific and personal. "My priorities are my own." "God has my heart, not you."

Point out the verse at the bottom of the page, Isaiah 55:9.

Q. How can this Scripture verse influence us just as powerfully as an ad for the latest jacket or video game?

A. It reminds us that no matter what the world says, God's way is better. No matter what thoughts we have in our minds, and no matter where they come from, God's ways are better. If we believe that, we can turn our heads away from the media and concentrate on thinking about the things God wants us to think about. We can make his priorities our priorities.

Visual images and auditory messages are everywhere. Unless you live in a cave or bury your head in the sofa cushions you can't avoid them. But you have the choice on what you decide to view (or to listen to) over and over again. You *can* walk out of a movie or throw away a magazine. You *can* choose not to buy the mature rated video game—even if you are seventeen.

Stand up and be counted. You'll need the right stuff, the life-changing Word of God if you are to make a stand and take back your life for Christ.

Close your time together with a prayer like this one.

Father, we want to see the world through your eyes. Help us turn our heads from the splashy influences that distract our attention from your holy ways. Help us to make the tough choice on our very next CD, DVD or movie ticket purchase. Give us the courage to look at our own motives honestly. In Jesus' name, amen.

WHAT IF?

Bible Truth:
Ease worry with prayer.

Bible Verse:
"Do not be anxious about anything, but in everything, by prayer and petition, with thanksgiving, present your requests to God" (Philippians 4:6).

Stuff: Bibles

LESSON NINE

BEGINNING

As you begin your devotional time together, ask God to help you consider the balance between worry and prayer in your life. Invite members of your group to share prayer requests if they are comfortable doing so. Have one or two volunteers pray aloud for the requests that have been shared.

Discuss:

Q. **What are the causes of teen worry? How much time do you spend worrying?**

A. Answers will vary. Ask what times of day they tend to worry most. Before school? During school? At home alone in the evening? In bed at night? And so on.

Q. **How does worry affect your physical health?**

A. You get a headache; your neck, back and chest get tight; you tend to get a dismal outlook on life. You can't focus on what you need to be doing because all you're thinking about is the thing you're worried about. You don't feel confident about things.

Summarize: **No matter what our worry factor is, the Bible has something to say about it.**

Optional Activity

Say, **I'm going to read a few simple statements. Hold up the number of fingers that indicates your personal "worry factor" for each. One is not worried at all, and five is worried sick.**

- **Keeping friendships**
- **Money**
- **Out-of-work parents**
- **Serious illness**
- **High school violence**
- **Two Ds on a semester grade report**
- **Paying for college**
- **Hurting someone you love**
- **Purpose in life**

MIDDLE

Have the group turn to "Up/In/Out" on page 46 of the Guys' section of *Acquire the Fire,* Issue 1. Ask a volunteer to read the Scripture passage.

Let's focus on the middle of this passage for a moment, starting with "Do not be anxious."

Q. What does God tell us not to do in this verse?

A. We're not to be anxious. That's means no worrying, no fretting, no second-guessing what might happen or expecting the worst all the time, no knots in the stomach, no sleepless nights, no biting nails.

Q. What does God tell us that we *should* do?

A. Pray and let him know what we need, and be thankful no matter what is going on. We can tell God anything.

Q. Why is it so hard for us to get this right?

A. Worrying is the natural human response, and we're all human. Sometimes we say with our mouths that we trust God, but we don't trust him in our hearts. We want to have control. We want to be sure of what's going to happen or know that things are going to happen just the way we want. Trusting God means letting him have control, even when we're not sure how things will turn out.

Trusting God means letting him have control, even if we're not sure how things will turn out.

Ask a volunteer to read the "Up" section. Discuss:

Q. Do you watch the news?

A. Answers will vary. Some teens keep track of the news more than others. Some of them are just not interested, but others may avoid watching the news because of the depressing stuff they see. If you need to prompt discussion further, ask about specific news items—war reports, murders, natural disasters. How do they feel when they see these things in the news?

Q. When you're worried, do you believe that God is near? Do you believe it with your heart?

A. Explore the difference between believing in your head, intellectually, that God is near and actually letting go of the worry because you believe with your heart. You believe *intellectually* because you know what the Bible says or you know what Christians are supposed to believe. However, you believe with your *heart* when you experience for yourself how God can help you with a real problem. How do feelings change when you reach the point of believing with your heart?

Q. God is in control. True or false?

A. Yes. If God is in control, you can let go. Whatever happens, God promises to work it out for good. If you trust God to work things out for good, then you release your worry to him.

Ask a volunteer to read the "In" section. The Israelites had good reason to be shaking in their boots. Pharaoh was not exactly a pushover when it came to the Israelite slaves leaving Egypt. But God made his people a promise, and he kept it. (If time allows, you may want to take a minute to read Exodus 12:31–42.)

Q. Bad stuff happens. How do you respond when it happens to you or someone you care about? How do you cope?

Whatever happens, God promises to work it out for good.

A. Most of us are disappointed but eventually move on. But some get angry or depressed and have a hard time recovering. They can't just get over it and move on. A lot of times we look for someone else to blame because we don't want to admit that anything we did might be the reason for the bad stuff. We blame other people, or we blame God.

Q. Is it possible for the peace of God to fill you in times of trouble and despair?

A. Yes. This is what he promises all who place their trust in him. Encourage teens to give personal, experiential answers. Don't hesitate to share one of your own—tell about something that made you anxious until you let go of the worry and trusted God to work it out. Be a model of the peace of God to help teens know it really does exist.

Ask a volunteer to read the "Out" section. Discuss:

Q. How do you respond when one of your friends is overwhelmed by worry?

A. Sometimes you don't know what to do to help, so maybe you do nothing and then feel bad about it later. You might try to say something encouraging or help the person see something good that's happening instead of focusing just on the bad stuff. Just be there.

Make prayer the rhythm of your life.

Q. God's peace is a promise that we carry with us throughout our lives. How can we let others know of this blessing?

A. Believe it yourself. Have a positive attitude even when things go wrong, so you can show God's peace at work in your own life. Find things to thank God for even when you have reason to be discouraged. Remind your friends of verses like Philippians 4:6 and pray with them. If the person is not a Christian, be a disciple for Christ and share his message of light, love, hope, and goodness.

God forbids us to worry and commands us to pray—even in times of suffering and doubt. Just think of the difference we could make in the world if we could just get this right. Make prayer the rhythm of your life.

END

Have the group turn to "Godfidential" on page 45 of the Guys' section of *Acquire the Fire*, Issue 1. Ask a volunteer to read this section aloud. Be sure to read Matthew 5:14–16 also.

Q. How can one teen make a difference? Can a single teen be a light onto the world?

A. Throughout time God used teenagers to do his work. The mother of Jesus was a teenager. If you care, your age will not matter to the person who needs your help. It could help point them to a relationship with Jesus, the true light. They would feel more hopeful and start thinking of ways they could solve their problems or trust that God will work things out in his time.

Q. Worry diminishes the light of Christ's love. Why?

A. You can't be a light to the world if you're hidden or burdened or overwhelmed with the darkness of sin and worry. When you serve others despite your pain and concerns, people will sense that you are working in partnership with a powerful Spirit far greater than your own abilities. God is Spirit. (John 4:24).

Q. Has your view of worry changed because of the discussion we've had today?

A. Answers will vary, but encourage the group to give genuine, thoughtful answers. Per God's command, worry is something that should not occupy our days.

Close your time together with a prayer like this one:

Lord, life is overwhelming at times, with too many questions and not enough answers. Too many "what ifs" and not enough people promises we can trust. But we know we can trust your promises. Indeed, your promises come wrapped in a godly peace. May we be lights of that peace to the world. In Jesus' name, amen.

GOD-ESTEEM

Bible Truth:
Choose peace over fear.

Bible Verse:
"Peace I leave with you; my peace I give you. I do not give to you as the world gives. Do not let your hearts be troubled and do not be afraid" (John 14:27).

Stuff: Bibles, paper, pencils

LESSON TEN

BEGINNING

As you begin your devotional time together, ask God to help you discover the source of true peace, his presence in your life. Invite members of your group to share prayer requests if they are comfortable doing so. Have one or two pray aloud for the requests that have been shared.

Discuss:

Q. If worry was a shape what form would it take? How does worry take shape in your life?

A. Mope around. Withdraw and stay in your room. Stop eating. Eat too much. Get cranky with other people. Have trouble sleeping. Sleep too much. Avoid the problem by ignoring it and doing something else. Avoid anything serious. The list goes on and on.

Q. Name something you worry about but wish you didn't have to.

A. Looks. Schoolwork. Family situations. Natural disasters. The future. College. Getting a job. Having friends. War. Being good at something. Fitting in. Having the right clothes. Weight. Crime near where you live. Having enough money.

MIDDLE

Have the group turn to "Girl Outstanding" on page 47 of the Girls' section of *Acquire the Fire,* Issue 1. Ask a volunteer to read this section aloud.

As you begin your discussion of this topic, make the point that worry and positive self-esteem are at odds with each other when it comes to being godly women and godly men. (The Guys' version of this devotional appears as "Mandatory" on page 47 of the Guys' section.)

Q. Where do you feel peer pressure? Hair? Hips? Biceps?

A. Pressure to have the right hair, the right body shape, to have athletic or academic ability. Pressure to excel at something you're competing in. Pressure to keep your grades up. Pressure not to do something stupid and disappoint your parents.

Pressure to have a girlfriend or boyfriend. Pressure to have sex or drink alcohol in order to fit in and have friends. Pressure to be as good at something as a sibling is. Pressure to do something your parents want you to do. Pressure to ace the SATs and get into the right college.

Q. Imagine a day without the pressure of worry. What joys or positives would take its place?

A. Most of us see the positives in other people a lot more easily than we see the positives in ourselves. We wish we were like so-and-so, instead of realizing the qualities we have in ourselves. If time allows, pass out paper and pencils have teens make confidential lists of the positives they see in themselves. Challenge them each to come up with at least five things they like about themselves. They don't have to share this with anyone.

We tend to compare the negatives in ourselves to the positives in others. Little wonder we come out on the losing end! Here's an idea. Take an hour this week and celebrate your strengths. No fault-finding, no nit-picking, no "I can't do anything right." Believe you are worthy and valuable and begin to see the joy of living in God's light.

Our true value comes from God, not from what others think of us.

Q. We're made in God's image (Genesis 1:27). What does this mean? How is it a very good thing?

A. When God created the first man and woman he declared them excellent in every way. The first couple was stamped with the image of God. In other words, they reflected God's personality and even his spirituality. True value comes from God, not from what others think of us. God made human beings as the crown of creation and he wants to have a relationship with them. We're valuable to God.

Q. So what is this thing called self-esteem? And how do I get a hold of it?

A. Your group may answer that self-esteem or positive self-worth comes from people believing in you or that it comes from being successful at something. Or it comes from knowing that you're doing your best to do the right thing. Yet, the ultimate source of our value rests in our godly creation, without having to prove anything. God-esteem comes from knowing what God thinks of us—infinite value—and the unfailing love he offers us.

Q. How can friends help?

A. Pray for others by name. Be a good listener. (Don't interrupt.) Give well-thought-out advice. Find time to share and be together. Turn off cell phones and give others your full attention. Don't judge or compare. Treat others the way you'd want to be treated.

It's not a sign of weakness to talk to someone who can help you figure things out. That's one of the great things about family and friendships—they help. Relationships are a God thing.

Q. Do you think it's all right to pray for better self-esteem? Explain.

A. Yes. God wants us to bring all our worries and concerns to him. And since God is the true source of self-esteem, it only makes sense to ask him for it.

Q. Name some qualities you see in people who have been energized and transformed by God's love

A. Inner peace. Humility. Loving toward others. Hopeful even in tough situations. Calm. Gentle. Happy. Forgiving. Satisfied.

END

Have everyone turn to "The Supernatural Power of Prayer" on page 48 of the Girls' section of *Acquire the Fire,* Issue 1.

Q. A troubled or broken heart is more than an expression. What are the warning signs of "heart" trouble?

A. You feel all jumbled up. Depressed. Can't concentrate. Like crying. Confused, don't know what to think or what to do.

Q. What is the difference between the peace that God gives and the peace that the world gives?

A. The world's peace is something that we think we can achieve on our own. If we can just figure everything out and get past the obstacles, we can find peace. But anything can happen to break the peace. The peace that God gives is a gift, and all we have to do is accept it. It's a deep-down, inside peace that nothing in the world can break.

Ask a volunteer to read the second prayer. Indeed, only you know what's happening within the walls of your home. You can personalize this prayer so that God will guide you when family situations create tension and unbalance in your life.

Ask a volunteer to read the last prayer. We spend enormous amounts of time and energy worrying about things we can't change—and things that don't need to be changed.

We're all individuals. We don't have to be like anyone else in order to be loved, feel loved, or to feel at peace. A perfect God made us and he gets things right. Offer to God in prayer the worries that burden your days.

Close your time together with a prayer like this one:

When we forget who you are, Father, we forget who we are. Pull us close. Remind us that evil has no hold on you. We release our worries to you so that we are free to experience unconditional love, peace and joy. In Jesus' name, amen.

The Word at Work Around the World

A vital part of Cook Communications Ministries is our international outreach, Cook Communications Ministries International (CCMI). Your purchase of this book, and of other books and Christian-growth products from Cook, enables CCMI to provide Bibles and Christian literature to people in more than 150 languages in 65 countries.

Cook Communications Ministries is a not-for-profit, self-supporting organization. Revenues from sales of our books, Bible curricula, and other church and home products not only fund our U.S. ministry, but also fund our CCMI ministry around the world. One hundred percent of donations to CCMI go to our international literature programs.

CCMI reaches out internationally in three ways:

· Our premier International Christian Publishing Institute (ICPI) trains leaders from nationally led publishing houses around the world.

· We provide literature for pastors, evangelists, and Christian workers in their national language.

· We reach people at risk—refugees, AIDS victims, street children, and famine victims—with God's Word.

Word Power, God's Power

Faith Kidz, RiverOak, Honor, Life Journey, Victor, NexGen — every time you purchase a book produced by Cook Communications Ministries, you not only meet a vital personal need in your life or in the life of someone you love, but you're also a part of ministering to José in Colombia, Humberto in Chile, Gousa in India, or Lidiane in Brazil. You help make it possible for a pastor in China, a child in Peru, or a mother in West Africa to enjoy a life-changing book. And because you helped, children and adults around the world are learning God's Word and walking in his ways.

Thank you for your partnership in helping to disciple the world. May God bless you with the power of his Word in your life.

For more information about our international ministries, visit www.ccmi.org.